The Best Gift Ever

The
Best Gift
Ever

Rebecca P. Small

Illustrated by Maria Jimenez

A publication of Family Reclamation Project

The Best Gift Ever
copyright © 2023 by Rebecca P. Small
www.reservoirofgrace.com
reservoirofgracefrp@gmail.com

Published by Family Reclamation Project
www.familyreclamationproject.com

Illustrations by Maria Jimenez
www.mariajostudio.com

iStockphoto.com, credit Brian A. Jackson, p. 12

Art assistance by John Molinero

Cover design by Mattaniah Small
www.clothespinmedia.com

All Scriptures are taken from the New Kings James Version (NKJV) of the Bible unless otherwise noted.
Copyright © 1982 by Thomas Nelson, Inc. Used by permission. All rights reserved.

Scripture quotations marked (NLT) are taken from the Holy Bible, New Living Translation, copyright © 1996, 2004, 2007 by Tyndale House Foundation. Used by permission of Tyndale House Publishers, Inc., Carol Stream, Illinois 60188. All rights reserved.

ALL RIGHTS RESERVED
No part of the publication may be reproduced, stored in a retrieval system, or transmitted in any form or by any means without prior written permission of the publisher.

ISBN: 978-1-7923-8385-4

Dedicated to Bob and Donna Steinbrugge:

Without your dedication and leadership in the Champions after-school program, I doubt if this book would ever have been written. Thank you both for your friendship, your example, your love for our community, and your deep desire to share life-changing truth.

Introduction

When our family moved to Brinnon, Washington, the church we attended had an after-school Bible club called "Champions" at the small local public school. I, along with two of my daughters, volunteered to help with the program. Eventually I became the Bible teacher for the three different age levels. Every year the church set aside one Sunday as "Champions Sunday." One year I was asked to share a flannelgraph lesson for that special Sunday, demonstrating to the church how I taught the children. Since I knew there might be parents who would come that Sunday who didn't usually attend church, I felt compelled to share the Gospel: the story of God's love for us and the best gift we've ever been offered or could ever receive.

In preparing the lesson, I selected various flannelgraph pieces to illustrate the concepts of the Gospel and then rehearsed it as I put the pieces on the flannel board. When I finished talking through the lesson the first time, some vital element seemed missing though I couldn't quite put my finger on it. I added a few more pieces to illustrate other truths and talked through it again. Still there was something missing. I pulled a few more pieces, praying for God's direction and enlightenment. This happened three or four times before the presentation at last seemed complete. At the end of the final rehearsal, tears were streaming down my face at the incredible gift God has made available to us through His Son, Jesus Christ. My heart was overflowing with worship for His love and grace, and for such a full salvation from sin.

Since that time, I have shared that same flannelgraph presentation at women's retreats and at mission conferences. Whenever I ask if I can share it, the response is usually skeptical. Flannelgraph? That's so old-school and certainly not for adults. Yet it is the adults who have been most moved by the visual presentation of the Gospel, often seeing for the first time elements of their salvation they had never understood before. Some have asked if I had the presentation in a form they could purchase to share with others. That request is what gave impetus for this book. Upon first glance, it appears to be a children's book, and it certainly can be used that way. But I hope it is more than that. I pray that this book with its simple illustrations can be used to share the amazing truths of the Gospel with anyone who has not yet found new life in Christ Jesus.

Table of Contents

1. The Bible: The Source of Truth   1

2. The Triune God: His Image in Creation   13

3. The Rebellion: Satan and His Kingdom   27

4. The Choice: The Knowledge of Good and Evil   33

5. The Promise: God's Gracious Provision   49

6. The Consequences: Sin and Its Effects   59

7. The Remedy: Jesus, the Promised Savior   67

8. The Gift: Righteousness and a New Creation   85

9. The Offer: The Great Exchange   95

An Invitation   113

Scripture References   117

Acknowledgements   138

1
The Bible:
The Source of Truth

The Bible: The Source of Truth

The Bible is the solid foundation upon which we build all of life and all of knowledge. It declares itself to be the absolute **TRUTH**. Coming from the very mouth of God, it explains the mysteries we all long to know and understand. The Bible reveals the heart of God and the plan of God, which He had conceived before time began.

John 17:17: Sanctify them by Your truth; Your Word is truth.

The Best Gift Ever

The story of God from the beginning of time is recorded in the Bible. It claims to be the very Word of God given to us through human hands. God used ordinary men to write His words, but it is not an ordinary book.

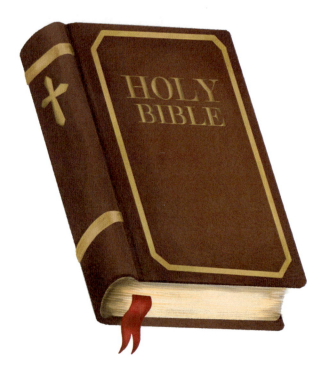

The Bible itself tells us that the words written in it are **inspired** by God, and that holy men of God spoke and wrote as they were moved by His Holy Spirit. You might say that the Bible is God's autobiography, His self-disclosure.

II Peter 1:21b: …holy men of God spoke as they were moved by the Holy Spirit.
II Timothy 3:16: All Scripture is given by inspiration of God…

The Bible: The Source of Truth

First and foremost, the Bible tells us about **God**, who He is and what He's done.

We cannot make up our own ideas about God. He wants to be known for who He is. He has spoken, revealing Himself through His Word, the Bible.

Jeremiah 9:24: ... "I am the Lord, exercising lovingkindness, justice, and righteousness in the earth, for in these I delight," says the Lord.

Time and time again, scientists, archaeologists, and anthropologists have doubted the authority and veracity of the Bible. They have scoffed at its accounts of the super-

natural and at its history and science. Yet time and time again, they have been proven wrong. The Bible withstands every test we give it.

The Bible is **true** not only about spiritual realities, history, and science, but also about the beginnings of the universe, our earth, and time.

If you don't believe what God says about the beginnings of the world, why should you believe anything else God says? But God, as the only eye-witness, has spoken and revealed the truth to us.

Isaiah 46:9-10: ...I am God, and there is no other; I am God, and there is none like Me, declaring the end from the beginning...

The opening chapters of Genesis are God's revelation about **origins**—not only the origin of the universe, including the earth and everything on it, but also the origins of all that governs and affects our daily lives. If the first 11 chapters of the Bible are changed or discredited, then the entire record of the Bible comes into question and its message is undermined.

The foundation of the whole message of the Bible is laid in those opening chapters, as well as the foundation for all of science, history, and civilization. Without the understanding of those chapters, the very underpinnings of society and knowledge collapse along with God's eternal plan.

The Best Gift Ever

For those first 11 chapters tell us:

- Why there are seasons, days, and years

- Why people are unique from all other living things

- Why we have a 7-day week

- Why we have marriage between one man and one woman

- Why there is evil in the world

- Why there is sickness, hardship, brokenness, sorrow, and death

---

Genesis 2:2: And on the seventh day God ended His work which He had done, and He rested on the seventh day from all His work which He had done.
Genesis 2:18: And the Lord God said, "It is not good that man should be alone; I will make him a helper comparable to him."

The Bible: The Source of Truth

- Why we wear clothing

- Why there are so many fossils

- Why the geological record looks the way it does

- Why we have different languages and nations

The rest of the Bible does not make sense apart from the truths revealed in the opening chapters of Genesis. Hopefully you will see why.

Genesis 3:21: Also for Adam and his wife the Lord God made tunics of skin, and clothed them.
Genesis 7:12, 20, 24: And the rain was on the earth forty days and forty nights... The waters prevailed fifteen cubits upward, and the mountains were covered...And the waters prevailed on the earth one hundred and fifty days.
Genesis 11:9: Therefore its name is called Babel, because there the Lord confused the language of all the earth; and from there the Lord scattered them abroad over the face of all the earth."

The Bible also tells us the truth about **ourselves** and the human condition.

Apart from the Bible we cannot understand or know ourselves, nor can we figure out our purpose.

Jeremiah 17:9: The human heart is the most deceitful of all things, and desperately wicked. Who really knows how bad it is? (NLT)

The Bible: The Source of Truth

The Bible explains all the basic **questions of life**:
- Who are we?
- Why do we think, feel, and act the way we do?
- Where did we come from?
- Where are we headed?
- What are we here for?
- What is the ultimate purpose of our lives?

Romans 11:36: For everything comes from Him and exists by His power and is intended for His glory. All glory to Him forever! (NLT)

God's character and His ways, as well as His redemptive plan and purpose, are all revealed in the Bible.

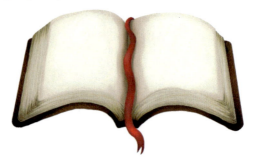

The outworking of His plan is called the **Gospel**, which means Good News. In fact, it is the best news about the best gift ever.

Colossians 1:19-20: For it pleased the Father that in Him [Jesus Christ] all the fullness should dwell, and by Him to reconcile all things to Himself, by Him, whether things on earth or things in heaven, having made peace through the blood of His cross.

2

The Triune God:

His Image in Creation

The Triune God: His Image in Creation

The Bible starts with these words:

The Hebrew word for God in that opening verse is

It is a plural word. Right at the outset God is telling us that He is **diversity within unity**.

The Bible reveals the God Elohim as trinitarian: one God manifest in three persons, the Father, the Son, and the Holy Spirit.

II Corinthians 13:14: The grace of the Lord Jesus Christ, and the love of God, and the communion of the Holy Spirit be with you all. Amen.

The opening verse of the Bible also tells us that the triune God is the **Creator** of all things:

The spiritual world,

the physical world,

and even the chronological world of history recorded throughout time.

The Bible tells us about all three worlds.

Colossians 1:16: For by Him [Jesus Christ] all things were created that are in heaven and that are on earth, visible and invisible, whether thrones or dominions or principalities or powers. All things were created through Him and for Him.

The Triune God: His Image in Creation

In the opening chapter of the Bible, we are told that God spoke the universe into existence. He created with His **words**. He commanded, and what He said came into being.

In fact, when scientists talk about the origins of the earth and the universe, they are really talking about history: what happened historically when the universe began.

Genesis 2:4: This is the history of the heavens and the earth when they were created, in the day that the Lord God made the earth and the heavens.

The creation of the world reflects the trinitarian nature of God. Without the Trinity, we would have a flat world; for God could not have created something more than He is Himself.

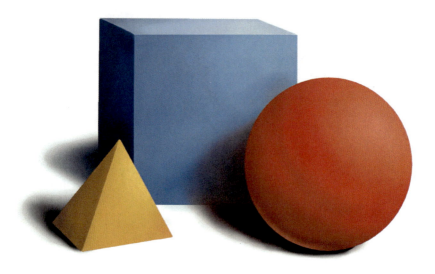

Trinity gives dimension to the universe and to our world. **Unity in diversity**, diversity in unity—Trinity is woven into the very fabric of everything around us.

Psalm 104:24: O Lord, how manifold are Your works! In wisdom You have made them all. The earth is full of Your possessions.
Psalm 97:6: The heavens declare His righteousness, and all the peoples see His glory.
Psalm 75:1: We give thanks to You, O God, we give thanks! For Your wondrous works declare that Your name is near.

Consider these amazing ways **Trinity** is embedded into our world: Triangles graph in waves.

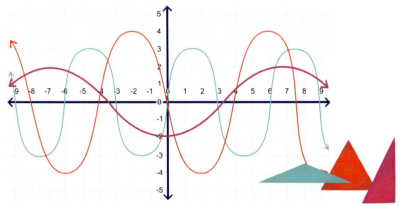

Sound comes to us in waves.

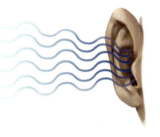

This means that everything we hear is Trinity audible.

Light also comes to us in waves.

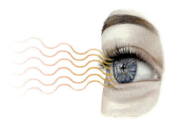

So everything we see is Trinity visible!

The truth of the trinitarian God is displayed all around us.

Psalm 111:2: The works of the Lord are great, studied by all who have pleasure in them.

The Best Gift Ever

From the Bible we learn that God reigns over a spiritual **kingdom**, which was to rule over the earth.

It is a glorious, eternal kingdom, one of light and life, full of all that is beautiful and good, desirable and satisfying.

Psalm 45:6: Your throne, O God, is forever and ever; a scepter of righteousness is the scepter of Your kingdom.
Psalm 103:19: The Lord has established His throne in heaven, and His kingdom rules over all.

The Triune God: His Image in Creation

And the Bible tells us that God is **love**. Within the Trinity, they shared perfect love, fellowship, and unity.

In order to display His glory and goodness, God planned a universe and a world that would reflect His character and truth. God, who has limitless love to share, made creatures upon whom He could lavish His love and with whom He could share His kingdom.

I John 4:7-8: Beloved, let us love one another, for love is of God, and everyone who loves is born of God and knows God. He who does not love does not know God, for God is love.

The Best Gift Ever

The crowning jewel of all God's creation was **humanity**, made in His own image. God did not speak man and woman into existence as He had the rest of creation, but He fashioned them with His own hands and breathed into them His own breath of life. And so man became a living soul.

This was the

First Adam

Genesis 2:7: And the Lord God formed man of the dust of the ground, and breathed into his nostrils the breath of life; and man became a living being.

22

The Triune God: His Image in Creation

The Gospel of Luke calls him the son (with a small *s*) of God because He was hand-fashioned by God and made in the likeness of God.

son of God

God saw that it was not good that Adam should be alone, so He created a woman to be Adam's counterpart. God formed Adam from the dust of the ground, but the woman was formed from a rib taken out of Adam's side.

Four times in two verses the Bible tells us that people are made in the likeness or **image of God**: "Then God said, 'Let Us make man in Our image, according to Our likeness... So God created man in His own image; in the image of God He created him, male and female."

Genesis 5:1-2: This is the book of the genealogy of Adam. In the day that God created man, He made him in the likeness of God. He created them male and female, and blessed them and called them Mankind in the day they were created.

Every person is created in the image of God. As God is trinitarian, so also **people are trinitarian**.

We have a spirit, a soul, and a body. Our spirit is what makes humanity entirely unique from all other created things. It is our spirit that connects us to God and enables us to commune with God. God created us to live out of our spirit in communion with Him so that His love, goodness, power, and wisdom could flow into our lives.

Our spirit was created to direct our soul according to the will and purposes of God. Even our soul is trinitarian: our mind, our will, and our emotions. Our soul was then to direct our body, but the command center was to be the spirit.

I Thessalonians 5:23: Now may the God of peace Himself sanctify you completely; and may your whole spirit, soul, and body be preserved blameless at the coming of our Lord Jesus Christ.

The Triune God: His Image in Creation

After God formed the man and woman, He gave them dominion over all the earth. They were created to be **God's partners**, ruling and reigning over all creation under God's authority.

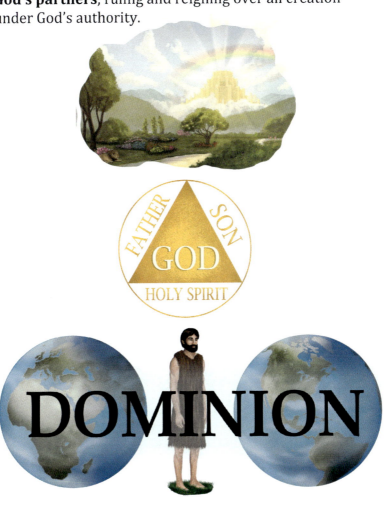

Genesis 1:28: Then God blessed them, and God said to them, "Be fruitful and multiply, fill the earth and subdue it, have dominion over the fish of the sea, over the birds of the air, and over every living thing that moves on the earth."

3

The Rebellion:

Satan and His Kingdom

The Rebellion: Satan and His Kingdom

God created other beings in the spiritual realm called **angels**.

These angels were to be His servants and messengers, serving people.

Psalm 148:2, 5: Praise Him, all His angels; praise Him, all His hosts! Let them praise the name of the Lord, for He commanded and they were created.

Hebrews 1:13-14: But to which of the angels has He ever said: "Sit at My right hand, till I make Your enemies Your footstool"? Are they not all ministering spirits sent forth to minister for those who will inherit salvation?

The Best Gift Ever

One of those angels rebelled. Perhaps as the angels watched God forming man in His own image, this angel became jealous; *he* wanted to be like God. And so started his rebellion. The Bible is not clear about the initial cause. But we are told that this angel's heart was lifted up in pride. He did not want to serve God. He wanted to BE God.

We now know this angel as the devil or **Satan.**

Isaiah 14:13-14: For you have said in your heart: "I will ascend into heaven, I will exalt my throne above the stars of God; I will also sit on the mount of the congregation, on the farthest sides of the north; I will ascend above the heights of the clouds, I will be like the Most High."
Luke 10:18: And He [Jesus] said to them, "I saw Satan fall like lightning from heaven."

The Rebellion: Satan and His Kingdom

Satan wanted to usurp God's rule and reign over the earth and establish his own kingdom. He rose up against God, persuading one-third of the angels to follow him in his rebellion. His very name means enemy or adversary, one who resists.

Satan is the antithesis of all that God is. His kingdom is one of eternal darkness and death. It is the exact **opposite** of God's kingdom. Rebellion against God can only lead to the opposite of God. We cannot rebel against God and His ways and still retain the qualities of His character and His kingdom.

Revelation 12:3-4, 9: And another sign appeared in heaven: behold, a great, fiery red dragon having seven heads and ten horns, and seven diadems on his heads. His tail drew a third of the stars of heaven and threw them to the earth...So the great dragon was cast out, that serpent of old, called the Devil and Satan, who deceives the whole world; he was cast to the earth, and his angels were cast out with him.

The rejection of God is also a rejection of all that He embodies and stands for.

Instead of love, Satan has only **hatred.** His goal is to distort and destroy those created in God's image by masquerading as an angel of light and truth. He pretends to offer well-being and freedom. In this way he seeks to win our allegiance, thinking he can thwart God's plan.

John 8:44: He was a murderer from the beginning, and does not stand in the truth, because there is no truth in him. When he speaks a lie, he speaks from his own resources, for he is a liar and the father of it.
II Corinthians 11:14: ..Satan himself transforms himself into an angel of light.

4

The Choice:

The Knowledge of Good and Evil

The Choice: The Knowledge of Good and Evil

God specifically designed the world as a place where people could **flourish** and be blessed. It was perfect and beautiful in every way, thriving under His kind and gracious rule and reign.

There was no pain, sadness, sickness, sorrow, or death.

Genesis 1:31: Then God saw everything that He had made, and indeed it was very good.

The Best Gift Ever

In a further display of creative genius, God planted a garden for the first man and woman. This beautiful environment in which they lived was filled with abundance. Right in the center of that garden, God planted **two trees**, the Tree of Life and the Tree of the Knowledge of Good and Evil.

Genesis 2:8-9: The Lord God planted a garden eastward in Eden, and there He put the man whom He had formed. And out of the ground the Lord God made every tree grow that is pleasant to the sight and good for food. The tree of life was also in the midst of the garden, and the tree of the knowledge of good and evil.

Genesis 2:15-17: Then the Lord God took the man and put him in the garden of Eden to tend and keep it. And the Lord God commanded the man, saying, "Of every tree of the garden you may freely eat; but of the tree of the knowledge of good and evil you shall not eat, for in the day that you eat of it you shall surely die."

The Choice: The Knowledge of Good and Evil

Couched within the gift and provision of the garden, God gave Adam one command.

God told Adam he could eat of all the trees in the garden, but of the Tree of the Knowledge of Good and Evil he was not to eat.

Along with the command, God also told him the consequences of disobedience:

> If he ate of that tree, he would surely **die**.

God was not threatening Adam—let's be very clear about that! He was simply telling him the truth. He was **warning** him out of love. God is the Creator and Author of life. In fact, the Bible tells us that He Himself is life, and His truth is life-giving. Therefore, to disobey Him can only and necessarily lead to death.

Disobedience to God's commands is the definition of sin, and the logical outcome of sin is death. It is the way the universe works.

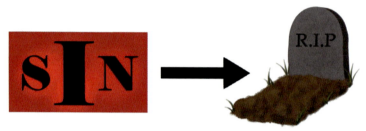

We cannot create our own definitions of what is right and wrong, defying what God has said, and still expect to have life. Only God and His ways lead to life.

Deuteronomy 30:15-18: See, I have set before you today life and good, death and evil, in that I command you today to love the Lord your God, to walk in His ways, and to keep His commandments, His statutes, and His judgments, that you may live...and the Lord your God will bless you....But if your heart turns away...I announce to you today that you shall surely perish...
Romans 6:23a: For the wages of sin is death...

The Choice: The Knowledge of Good and Evil

God did not put the Tree of the Knowledge of Good and Evil off in a corner with a high fence around it, to ensure Adam and his wife would not make a wrong choice to eat from it.

They had only one protection: The TRUTH based on the Word of God. Would they trust His Word and obey? Out of love for them, God was giving them a **choice** to walk with Him in obedience and love or to refuse His counsel and disobey. Love must be freely given, or it is not love at all.

 CHOICE

Genesis 2:9: The tree of life was also in the midst of the garden, and the tree of the knowledge of good and evil.
Proverbs 3:5-6: Trust in the Lord with all your heart and lean not on your own understanding. In all your ways acknowledge Him and He shall direct your paths.

The Best Gift Ever

As the adversary of God, Satan is always looking for ways to usurp God's throne. Seeing an opportunity to expand his kingdom and garner more subjects, Satan entered the garden in the form of a **serpent**. Evidently this serpent looked quite different from what we know today because God later cursed him to crawl on his belly.

The real conquest was not just humanity; the **dominion** of the earth was at stake here.

Because God had given the dominion of the world to Adam, only Adam could transfer that authority to another. World domination was exactly what Satan was after.

Genesis 3:14: So the Lord God said to the serpent; "Because you have done this, you are cursed more than all cattle, and more than every beast of the field; on your belly you shall go, and you shall eat dust all the days of your life.
I John 5:19: We know that we are of God, and the whole world lies under the sway of the wicked one.

The Best Gift Ever

However, Satan did not go after Adam directly. He waited to enter the garden until God had fashioned the woman and brought her to Adam as his perfect companion. Instead of speaking to the man, Satan chose to reach Adam through the woman.

His strategy was quite devious. First, he planted a **seed of doubt** in the woman's mind about the goodness of God: "Did God really say that you can't eat from all the trees in the garden?" He tried to make the abundance God had given look like it was not enough, as though they were being deprived. Through subtle suggestion, Satan caused her to feel that God was withholding something from them.

Doubting the goodness of God is always the first step toward sin.

Genesis 3:1: Now the serpent was more cunning than any beast of the field which the Lord God had made. And he said to the woman, "Has God indeed said, 'You shall not eat of every tree of the garden'?"

The Choice: The Knowledge of Good and Evil

The enemy of our souls uses a 3-step tactic in his **deception** process. Once we begin to doubt God's goodness, then Satan can directly lie, saying the opposite of what God has said: "You will not surely die!" Who is the woman now to believe? She had never been lied to before.

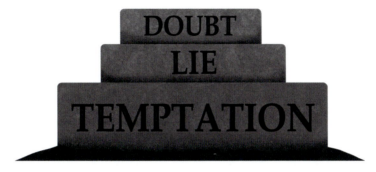

Then Satan tempted her with the very thing she already had from God: "God knows that in the day you eat of it, you will be like God." She already *was* like God. This is how God had created her! The only thing she hadn't experienced, but which God knew about, was evil. God wanted to spare mankind from that knowledge.

Beyond all doubt, Satan's words and God's words are clearly contradictory; she cannot believe both. A choice has to be made.

Genesis 3:4-5: Then the serpent said to the woman, "You will not surely die. For God knows that in the day you eat of it your eyes will be opened, and you will be like God, knowing good and evil."

The Best Gift Ever

As she considered her options, she saw that the fruit was good to eat, it certainly looked lovely, and she thought it could make her **more** than she was.

So she took of the fruit and gave some to her husband who was there with her.

Genesis 3:6: So when the woman saw that the tree was good for food, that it was pleasant to the eyes, and a tree desirable to make one wise, she took of its fruit and ate. She also gave to her husband with her, and he ate.

The Choice: The Knowledge of Good and Evil

But here's the subtle deception: Satan enticed Adam and his wife to believe that they were becoming independent and in control, making their own decisions, obeying no one but themselves, looking out for themselves, and following their own will. But whose will were they really following? Who were they really obeying? Correct. Satan.

They had not become independent at all, but rather they had **transferred** their loyalty out of God's spiritual kingdom into Satan's kingdom.

Ephesians 2:1-3: ...you once walked according to the course of this world, according to the prince of the power of the air, the spirit who now works in the sons of disobedience, among whom also we all once conducted ourselves in the lusts of our flesh, fulfilling the desires of the flesh and of the mind, and were by nature children of wrath...

The Best Gift Ever

They did become more than they had been. What was added to their lives was all that we hate about ourselves and our world. We all struggle with these things and fight hard to eradicate them:

- Anger
- Selfishness
- Hatred
- Bitterness
- Laziness
- Covetousness...
- Injustice
- Oppression
- Sickness
- Pain
- Death
- Sorrow...

Immediately they realized their **shame** and hid from the God who had lovingly created them. They tried to cover themselves, but no attempts are sufficient to cover up or make up for the disobedience already committed.

Genesis 3:7-8: Then the eyes of both of them were opened, and they knew that they were naked, and they sewed fig leaves together and made themselves coverings...and Adam and his wife hid themselves from the presence of the Lord God among the trees of the garden.

The Choice: The Knowledge of Good and Evil

Because God's heart is full of love, the disobedience of the first man and woman did not cause Him to shun them or destroy them. Instead, God came into the garden and sought them. He asked three questions. The first question is very telling:

1. "Where are you?"

Where did they go? They were still in the garden, but now they were hiding from God. Because they had made the choice to reject God's rule and reign, fear now dominated their relationship with God.

The closeness, the communication, the **spirit connection was gone**.

Genesis 3:9-10: Then the Lord God called to Adam and said to him, "Where are you?" So he said, "I heard Your voice in the garden, and I was afraid because I was naked and I hid myself."

And these were the second and third questions:

    2. "Who told you that you were naked?"

Their sin brought a self-awareness of shame and guilt.

    3. "Have you eaten from the tree which I commanded you not to eat?"

God didn't ask these questions because He didn't know the answers. Rather, He asked in order to elicit their response and confession.

CONFESSION

is the first step toward
reconciliation and restoration.

Psalm 32:5: I acknowledged my sin to You, and my iniquity I have not hidden. I said, "I will confess my transgressions to the Lord," and You forgave the iniquity of my sin.

5

The Promise:
God's Gracious Provision

The Promise: God's Gracious Provision

This act of disobedience brought a series of judgments into the world. After Adam and his wife confessed their guilt, God described the consequences of what they had done. Right in the middle of those pronouncements, God also promised a **Savior** who would one day crush Satan's head and reverse all the devastation of sin and death.

This Savior would restore creation to its original design.

Genesis 3:15: And I will put enmity between you and the woman, and between your seed and her Seed; He shall bruise your head, and you shall bruise His heel.

The Best Gift Ever

God told the serpent that the promised Savior would be born of a woman.

Do you see the kindness of God in that promise? Rather than condemn the woman for being the one who brought sin into the world, God was going to use her to usher in His promised salvation!

EVE = "The mother of all living"

Adam took hold of the **promise** by faith and named his wife Eve, which means "living." God had just declared that their sin brought the curse of death upon all mankind. Yet, Adam didn't call his wife "the mother of all who will die," but rather "the mother of all who will live."

Genesis 3:20: And Adam called his wife's name Eve because she was the mother of all living.

The Promise: God's Gracious Provision

On the basis of Adam's confession of faith, God provided an atoning sacrifice, a **substitute** to take the death Adam and Eve deserved. The Bible tells us that God made clothing for them out of animal skins. In order for their clothing to be made from animal skins, the animal had to die.

God had told Adam that disobedience to His command would result in death.

Genesis 3:21: Also for Adam and his wife, the Lord God made tunics of skin, and clothed them.
Ezekiel 18:20: The soul who sins shall die.

The Best Gift Ever

Sin by its very nature brings death to the one who has sinned. In order to spare a person from the death they have brought upon themselves, an **innocent victim** with no sin of its own must die in their place. This substitute death is the price of redemption to buy us back from the dominion of the enemy.

We are not told what kind of animal, or how many, God used to clothe Adam and Eve. Perhaps several had to be killed. Quite likely they were lambs because God is constantly painting pictures for us, using metaphors to explain His redemptive plan.

Leviticus 17:11: For the life of the flesh is in the blood, and I have given it to you upon the altar to make atonement for your souls; for it is the blood that makes atonement for the soul.
Hebrews 9:22b: For without the shedding of blood, there is no forgiveness. (NLT)

The Promise: God's Gracious Provision

Many years later on the night of the first Passover when God was delivering the Israelites out of Egypt, He told each household to kill a lamb, unspotted and unblemished, and to put the blood on the top and sides of their doors, forming the outline of a cross.

And when John the Baptizer first pointed out Jesus as the Messiah, he said, "Behold, the **Lamb of God** who takes away the sin of the world."

Exodus 12:3, 5-7, 13: On the tenth of this month every man shall take for himself a lamb…Your lamb shall be without blemish…Then the whole assembly of the congregation of Israel shall kill it at twilight. And they shall take some of the blood and put it on the two doorposts and on the lintel of the houses…Now the blood shall be a sign for you on the houses…And when I see the blood, I will pass over you; and the plague shall not be on you to destroy you…
John 1:29: The next day John saw Jesus coming toward him and said, "Behold, the Lamb of God who takes away the sin of the world."

The Best Gift Ever

The sacrifice of the animals used to make Adam and Eve's clothing was the **first death** the world had ever known.

This is why the Genesis record is completely incompatible with the theory of evolution. Evolution presupposes millions of years of death before man comes on the stage of history. But the Bible states,

"By man came sin, and from sin came death."

These two lines of thinking about origins and death are contradictory to one another.

Sadness, sickness, sorrow, tragedy, and death have been the result of the brokenness of our world because of sin. Sin is disobedience to God based on a refusal to believe His Word. It is a choice to trust ourselves rather than to trust God. This is the cause of all the evil and death in the entire history of the world.

Romans 5:12: Therefore, just as through one man sin entered the world, and death through sin, and thus death spread to all men, because all sinned…

The Promise: God's Gracious Provision

Because of God's love for mankind, He did not want them to live forever in a state of sorrow and death. To prevent Adam and Eve from eating of the **Tree of Life**, He sent them out of the garden and placed an angel with a flaming sword at its entrance.

Genesis 3:24: So He drove out the man; and He placed cherubim at the east of the garden of Eden, and a flaming sword which turned every way, to guard the way to the tree of life.

6

The Consequences:

Sin and Its Effects

The Consequences: Sin and Its Effects

So, what all has transpired? We have seen that Adam and Eve made a choice to obey Satan rather than God.

The **dominion** God had given to man, Adam had now handed over to Satan.

They had transferred their loyalty out of God's kingdom into Satan's kingdom. Their entire identity was changed.

I John 5:19: We know that we are of God, and the whole world lies under the sway of the wicked one.

The Best Gift Ever

With that act of **disobedience** to God, sin entered the world for the first time. The world was plunged into spiritual darkness.

When we choose to believe a lie rather than the truth of God's Word, we are choosing to believe that we know better than God. By usurping God's authority and taking that authority upon ourselves, our lives become self-focused and self-centered.

Sin is putting myself at the center of the universe—what *I* want and what *I* need—instead of trusting God and what He has said.

Romans 3:23: For all have sinned and fall short of the glory of God.
Romans 5:19a: ...as by one man's disobedience many were made sinners...

The Consequences: Sin and Its Effects

Their sin initiated a trinity of death. The spirit of mankind died.

1. The spirit connection was severed, and they were now **separated from God**, the Author of life. The Bible says we are dead in our transgressions and sins.

2. Their soul now revolved around self and became completely sin saturated, affecting all three parts of the soul:

   - their minds
     (how they thought),

   - their emotions
     (how they felt),

   - and their will
     (how they made their decisions).

3. And a cellular change happened in their bodies, which began the process of degeneration, leading to physical death.

Isaiah 59:2: But your iniquities have separated you from your God; and your sins have hidden His face from you…

The Best Gift Ever

We were created to live out of our spirit by faith in the directives from God with our spirit controlling our mind, will, and emotions. Our spirit-controlled soul was then to direct the body.

When sin entered the world, the order of spirit, soul, and body was reversed and turned **upside-down**. Instead of living out of our spirit, our spirit was now dead. The connection with God was broken, and the soul began taking its directives from the body.

Romans 8:5-8, 13: For those who live according to the flesh set their minds on the things of the flesh...for to be carnally minded is death...because the carnal mind is enmity against God, for it is not subject to the law of God, nor indeed can be. So then, those who are in the flesh cannot please God...For if you live according to the flesh you will die.

The Consequences: Sin and Its Effects

From then on, all who have been born through Adam, in his line, have been **born in sin**.

Because of our sin, Satan has legal claim over our lives.

Our spirit is dead, the soul is controlled by whatever the body wants, and the body will eventually die.

---

1 Corinthians 15:22: For as in Adam all die…

The Best Gift Ever

We have all broken God's Law in multiple ways.

We have all chosen the path of disobedience to God, distrusting the truth and goodness of His commands. All of us have gone our own way. We have all created our own standards. Like Adam and Eve, we have all eaten from the tree of the knowledge of good and evil, choosing for ourselves what is right and wrong. We have put our faith in our own ability to decide what is acceptable and what is not.

But God has spoken and has revealed to us what is best for us. We cannot violate His commands without **consequences**. As breakers of God's law, we all deserve to die.

Isaiah 53:6: All we like sheep have gone astray; we have turned, every one, to his own way...

66

7

The Remedy:

Jesus, the Promised Savior

The Remedy: Jesus, the Promised Savior

God could have washed His hands of the human race, but He had promised a **Redeemer**, One who would rescue us out of Satan's domain.

He would be the innocent substitute victim, the One who would reverse our brokenness. God was not taken by surprise at Adam and Eve's sin. In fact, the Bible says He had set a plan in place to reverse the damage of sin before He ever began to create.

1 Peter 1:20: He [Christ] indeed was foreordained before the foundation of the world, but was manifest in these last times for you.

The Best Gift Ever

He wasn't finished with those He had created in His own image. He was just beginning to reveal the full nature of His loving character. His heart will always overflow with grace toward those created in His image.

When the time was right, God sent His own **Son**.

Like Adam, this holy Child is called the

SON OF GOD

(with a capital S).

However, unlike Adam, He was not *fashioned by* God, but *begotten of* God.

Galatians 4:4: But when the fullness of the time had come, God sent forth His Son, born of a woman, born under the law...

The Remedy: Jesus, the Promised Savior

When an angel was sent to a young woman named Mary, he announced that she would have a son. He told her that the Holy Spirit would come upon her and that her baby boy would be called the Son of the Highest.

This Child would be born of a **virgin**.

His Father was God.

He is called the

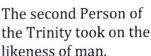

The second Person of the Trinity took on the likeness of man.

Luke 1:31-32, 35: Then the angel said to her, "Behold, you will conceive in your womb and bring forth a Son, and shall call His name Jesus. He will be great, and will be called the Son of the Highest...The Holy Spirit will come upon you, and the power of the Highest will overshadow you; therefore, also, that Holy One who is to be born will be called the Son of God."
John 1:14, 18: And the Word became flesh and dwelt among us, and we beheld His glory, the glory as of the only begotten of the Father, full of grace and truth...No one has seen God at any time. The only begotten Son, who is in the bosom of the Father, He has declared Him.
John 3:16: For God so loved the world that He gave His only begotten Son...

The Best Gift Ever

Not long after this announcement to Mary, the angel appeared to Joseph, her fiancé, in a dream and told him three very important things:

1. The Child Mary bore was conceived by the Holy Spirit

2. The Child was to be named Jesus because He would save His people from their sins. The name Jesus means "God is salvation."

3. The Child's birth fulfilled the prophecy of Isaiah that said the virgin's Son would be called **Immanuel**, which means God with us.

Jesus was born in the family line of God and He Himself was God.

Matthew 1:23: Behold, the virgin shall be with child, and bear a Son, and they shall call His name Immanuel, which is translated, "God with us."
John 1:1: In the beginning was the Word, and the Word was with God, and the Word was God.

The Remedy: Jesus, the Promised Savior

It's very important to understand that Jesus was not born in the family line of Adam. He did not inherit the sin nature of Adam. This is why the virgin birth is essential to the message of God's plan. If He were to rescue mankind from sin and its effects, He would have to be **without sin** Himself.

I Corinthians 15:45, 47: And so it is written, "The first man Adam became a living being." The last Adam became a life-giving spirit...The first man was of the earth, made of dust; the second Man is the Lord from heaven.

The Best Gift Ever

Jesus was the **Christ**, which is the Greek translation of the Hebrew word **Messiah**. Messiah means "sent One" or "anointed One." All the way back in Genesis 3 after the first sin, God had promised He would send Someone to destroy Satan. This is the One the world had been waiting for throughout the long ages of history.

John 4:25-26: The woman said to Him, "I know that Messiah is coming" (who is called Christ). "When He comes, He will tell us all things." Jesus said to her, "I who speak to you am He."

The Remedy: Jesus, the Promised Savior

He is also called the **Savior of the world**, the One who would save the world from its sin and destruction. As God had promised, Jesus would crush Satan's head and reverse all the horrific damage caused by sin. Through the sacrifice of Himself as the innocent victim, He would make a way for us not only to be restored to God's original design but also to be clothed in His own perfection. The penalty for the sins committed by everyone in the whole world would be placed upon Him.

John 4:42: Then they said to the woman, "Now we believe, not because of what you said, for we ourselves have heard Him and we know that this is indeed the Christ, the Savior of the world."

The Best Gift Ever

When Jesus was being baptized in the Jordan River by John the Baptizer, the **Holy Spirit** came down from heaven in the form of a dove. The Spirit descended upon Jesus and rested upon Him, anointing and empowering Him to teach and perform miracles just as the Bible had prophesied hundreds of years before.

Matthew 3:16: When He had been baptized, Jesus came up immediately from the water; and behold, the heavens were opened to Him, and He saw the Spirit of God descending like a dove and alighting upon Him.

And the voice of God spoke audibly from heaven, saying,

"This is My beloved Son, in whom I am well pleased."

The dove and the voice of God were the **signs** proving that Jesus was the One God had promised to send. This is He.

The Trinity was working together in unity to reveal the one true God and to bring about the salvation of mankind.

Matthew 3:17: And suddenly a voice came from heaven, saying, "This is My Beloved Son, in whom I am well pleased."

Jesus never broke God's Law. He always believed and trusted that what God said was good and right. He always walked in obedience to God.

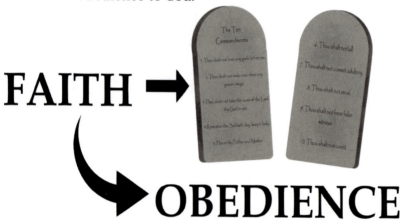

He was perfect, without any sin.

The name that Jesus most often used for Himself was not Son of God, but **Son of Man**. Why? Because as the Son of God, He was showing us exactly what God is like; but as the Son of Man, He was showing us what true man was intended to be like. Here was the true image-bearer of God.

I John 3:5: And you know that He was manifested to take away our sins, and in Him there is no sin.
Hebrews 4:15: For we do not have a High Priest who cannot sympathize with our weaknesses, but was in all points tempted as we are, yet without sin.

The Remedy: Jesus, the Promised Savior

Yes. Look at Jesus. This is real, authentic man showing us how God originally designed us to be. He fully lived in connection with God the Father through the Holy Spirit within His spirit. This is why Jesus says repeatedly in the Gospel of John,

- "I only do those things that I receive from My Father."
- "I only say those things the Father tells Me to say."
- "I do nothing apart from what My Father gives Me to do."

He is **true man**, living out of His spirit in continual, unhindered relationship with God.

John 8:29: And He who sent Me is with Me. The Father has not left Me alone, for I always do those things that please Him.

The Best Gift Ever

In obedience to the Father's will, Jesus went to the cross. The night before He died, He prayed, "Not My will, but Yours be done." Death was not something that happened to Him as it does to us. Rather, He chose to willingly lay down His life in trusting obedience to God His Father. Jesus Himself said, "No one takes My life from Me; I lay it down of My own accord."

John the Baptizer had called Him the **Lamb of God**, who takes away the sin of the world. The innocent victim killed to cover the sin of Adam and Eve found prophetic fulfillment in Christ on the cross. And like the Passover lambs, Jesus was unspotted and without blemish.

John 10:11, 18: "I am the good shepherd. The good shepherd gives His life for the sheep...This command I have received from My Father.
I Peter 1:18-19: ...knowing that you were not redeemed with corruptible things, like silver or gold, from your aimless conduct received by tradition from your fathers, but with the precious blood of Christ, as of a lamb without blemish and without spot.
Isaiah 53:5-6: But He was wounded for our transgressions, He was bruised for our iniquities; the chastisement for our peace was upon Him, and by His stripes we are healed... and the Lord has laid on Him the iniquity of us all.

The Remedy: Jesus, the Promised Savior

We have seen that the penalty of sin is death. But because Jesus had no sin, death had no claim on Him. Death cannot hold a person who has been perfectly righteous, fully obeying God and His Word. Righteousness can never lead to death.

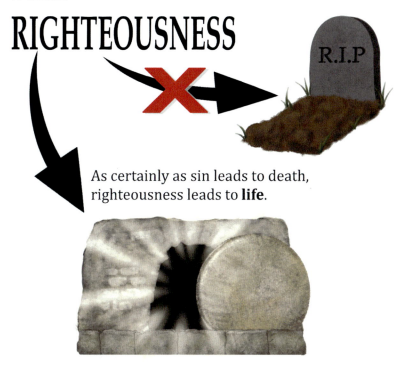

As certainly as sin leads to death, righteousness leads to **life**.

Since death could not claim Him, Christ rose from the dead, victorious over sin and death. His resurrection proved His innocence and His power over death. It is the assurance that His sacrifice on our behalf was accepted by God. The death and resurrection of Jesus Christ broke Satan's dominion over our lives.

Acts 2:23-24: Christ, being delivered by the determined purpose and foreknowledge of God, you have taken by lawless hands, have crucified, and put to death; whom God raised up, having loosed the pains of death, because it was not possible that He should be held by it.

The Best Gift Ever

Shortly before going to the cross, Jesus said, "Now the ruler of this world will be cast out." Since God had given the dominion of the earth to mankind, only another man could take it back. The first Adam forfeited the dominion to Satan. Christ as the **Last Adam**, the perfect man, took back the dominion of the world from Satan. Through His willing obedience, even to death on a cross, He destroyed the authority of Satan over mankind by bearing the punishment our sins deserved.

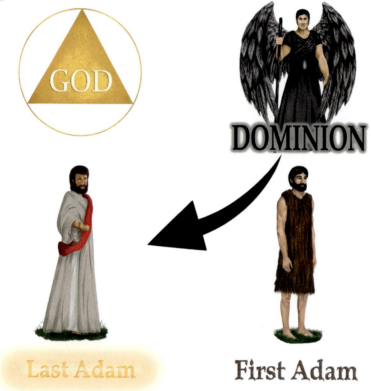

At the cross, Satan was dethroned, and his power was broken forever.

Matthew 28:18: And Jesus came and spoke to them, saying, "All authority has been given to Me in heaven and on earth."

The Remedy: Jesus, the Promised Savior

Jesus has rightly won the dominion that no one will ever be able to take from Him. God revealed to Daniel, one of the Old Testament prophets, that One like the Son of Man will one day come with the clouds of heaven. He will approach the throne of God and be given dominion, glory, and a kingdom. All peoples, nations, and languages will serve Him. His dominion is an **everlasting dominion**, which shall not pass away, and His kingdom the one which shall not be destroyed.

When all His enemies—even death itself—have been done away with, He will once again restore the earth to righteousness and love as God originally intended.

Daniel 7:13-14: I was watching in the night visions, and behold, One like the Son of Man, coming with the clouds of heaven! He came to the Ancient of Days, and they brought Him near before Him. Then to Him was given dominion and glory and a kingdom, that all peoples, nations, and languages should serve Him. His dominion is an everlasting dominion, which shall not pass away, and His kingdom the one which shall not be destroyed.

The Best Gift Ever

Before going to the cross, Jesus had told His disciples, "It is better for you if I go away; for if I go, I will send the Holy Spirit to you." He assured them He would not leave them alone. They would still have His Presence through the Holy Spirit who would be with them and in them forever.

After His resurrection, Jesus remained on earth for forty days. He appeared to His disciples several times, proving to them beyond all doubt that He truly was alive. Although the resurrection was astounding and world-altering, it was not the end goal of God's purpose for sending His Son.

Before Jesus ascended to heaven, He told His disciples to wait until the **Promise of the Father** was sent to them. For ten days they waited and prayed. Then the Holy Spirit came upon them with great power. The third Person of the Trinity came to live inside them! This was the same Spirit who had given Jesus power to fully obey God the Father.

The ultimate plan of God before time began had found its fulfillment: God had come to dwell with and in His people.

Luke 24:51: Now it came to pass, while He blessed them, that He was parted from them and carried up into heaven.
John 16:7: "Nevertheless I tell you the truth, it is to your advantage that I go away; for if I do not go away, the Helper will not come to you; but if I depart, I will send Him to you."

8

The Gift:

Righteousness and a New Creation

The Gift: Righteousness and a New Creation

The cross of Christ is the centerpiece of history.

Through Christ's death on the cross,

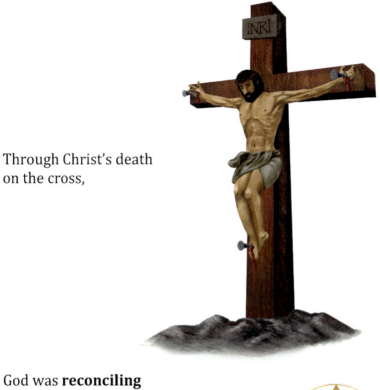

God was **reconciling** the world to Himself.

II Corinthians 5:19: God was in Christ reconciling the world to Himself, not imputing their trespasses to them...

The Best Gift Ever

Reconciling means

- to repair a broken relationship,
- to resolve the problem that caused the broken relationship,
- and to restore the friendship.

Our sins cut us off from God. When the sins of the world were laid on Jesus, He cried out, "My God, My God, why have You forsaken Me." For the first time in all eternity, God the Father and God the Son were torn apart, Jesus not only took our sins, but He also bore our separation from God.

Jesus came to reunite us with God through His death on the cross.

By paying the price for our sins, Jesus Christ made a way for us to come back to God and have a **restored relationship** with Him.

Romans 5:10: ...when we were enemies we were reconciled to God through the death of His Son...

The Gift: Righteousness and a New Creation

Because of what Jesus has done in obedience to the Father, God can now offer us a gift that gives us complete salvation from sin. Romans 5:17 tells us what that free gift is. It is the gift of His very own righteousness, a **new creation** within.

RIGHTEOUSNESS

BELIEVE

All we have to do is what Jesus did: Believe God's Word. When we trust what God has done for us in Christ, we receive this free gift of God.

Romans 5:17: For if by the one man's offense death reigned through the one, much more those who receive abundance of grace and of the gift of righteousness will reign in life through the One, Jesus Christ. **Acts 16:30-31:** And he brought them out and said, "Sirs, what must I do to be saved?" So they said, "Believe on the Lord Jesus Christ, and you will be saved, you and your household."

The Best Gift Ever

When we receive God's free gift of salvation from sin, three **identity transformations** occur.

1. We are transferred out of Satan's kingdom back into God's kingdom. We are no longer children of Adam or children of the devil.

Colossians 1:13: He has delivered us from the power of darkness and conveyed us into the kingdom of the Son of His love.

The Gift: Righteousness and a New Creation

2. Our spirit is reborn. We have now become **children of God**, having the seed or spiritual DNA of Christ within us.

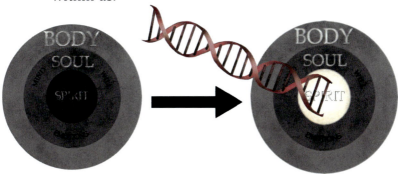

3. We have restored communion with God. The separation is gone. The love and goodness of the Father, the obedience and righteousness of Jesus, and the wisdom and life-giving power of the Spirit are all available to us. In short, all the glory of the Trinity flows into our lives through our renewed connection with God.

We have been given a whole new identity.

John 1:12-13: But as many as received Him (Jesus Christ), to them He gave the right to become children of God, to those who believe in His name, who were born, not of blood, nor of the will of the flesh, nor of the will of man, but of God.

The Best Gift Ever

Besides the three identity transformations, the gift of righteousness is itself trinitarian. In order for us to become truly righteous as God is, three things have to happen.

1. First of all, we have **forgiveness** through His blood. When Jesus cried out on the cross, "It is finished," He was announcing that our sin debt was paid in full for all eternity: past, present, and future.

Our sin was placed on Christ and nailed to the cross. Romans 4 says, "He was delivered over to death for our offenses." Our slate is wiped clean. We are brought back to where Adam and Eve started before the Fall: Innocent.

Ephesians 1:7: In Him we have redemption through His blood, the forgiveness of sins, according to the riches of His grace.

The Gift: Righteousness and a New Creation

Romans 4 goes on to say that Christ "was raised for our justification." Christ's resurrection proves His sacrifice was sufficient and accepted by God. The penalty for our sin has been paid and God is just in justifying us.

2. **Justification** is the second gift of righteousness, and it is far more than "just as if I'd never sinned," as some people like to define it. Justification is having the very righteousness of Christ credited to us. In other words, it's "just as if I'd always done the right thing at the right time in the right way for the right reasons."

God has not just taken us eternally out of our sin debt, but He has made us eternally as righteous as Christ, the very Son of God Himself! He has removed our shame and lavished honor upon us by giving us the riches of His perfect character. This is far better, far more than Adam and Eve ever had in the garden before the Fall.

Romans 4:25-5:1: [He—Jesus our Lord] was delivered up because of our offenses, and was raised because of our justification. Therefore, having been justified by faith, we have peace with God through our Lord Jesus Christ.

93

The Best Gift Ever

Yet we may have all our sins erased and be fully covered in Christ's righteousness and still not have the power to live and walk in obedience to God every day. So God gave us the third gift of righteousness.

> 3. He has put His **Spirit** in our hearts. The same Spirit who lived in Jesus and empowered Him to walk in perfect obedience to the Father has now been imparted to us. He has implanted His Spirit in our spirit. It is His Spirit within us who gives us the desire and the power to obey.

His Spirit gives us full 24/7 communion with God and access to God. All that God is He wants to impart to us through the Holy Spirit residing in us. It doesn't get any better or closer than that!

John 14:16-17: "And I will pray the Father, and He will give you another Helper, that He may abide with you forever—the Spirit of truth, whom the world cannot receive, because it neither sees Him nor knows Him; but you know Him, for He dwells with you and will be in you."

Philippians 2:13: For it is God who works in you both to will and to do for His good pleasure.

9

The Offer:

The Great Exchange

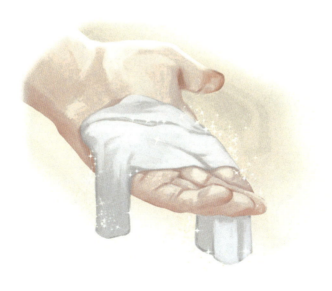

The Offer: The Great Exchange

Just like in the garden, God again places before us a **choice**.

We can receive   OR   stay where we are with

- Christ
- Pardon
- Life

- Satan
- Sin
- Death

CHOICE

Deuteronomy 30:19-20: I call heaven and earth as witnesses today against you, that I have set before you life and death, blessing and cursing; therefore choose life that both you and your descendants may live; that you may love the Lord your God, that you may obey His voice, and that you may cling to Him, for He is your life...

The Best Gift Ever

God does not force or even coerce. Because love and obedience must be freely given, He simply tells us the truth and offers us a choice.

Satan doesn't offer us choices. While making us think we've chosen independently, he manipulates and **deceives** us with lies into doing his will. Using force and fear, he threatens us and coerces us into doing his will.

The fact that God gave Adam and Eve a free choice proves that a loving God is in charge of the universe.

CHOICE

Joshua 24:15: Choose for yourselves this day whom you will serve.

The Offer: The Great Exchange

Jesus is the only way out of Adam's sinful line and back to God.

Jesus Himself said, "I am the Way, the Truth, and the Life." He went on to say that no one can come to the Father except through Him.

Peter, one of Jesus' closest disciples, told the religious leaders of his day that there is no other name under heaven—**no other name** in all the world but Jesus—that can make us right with God again.

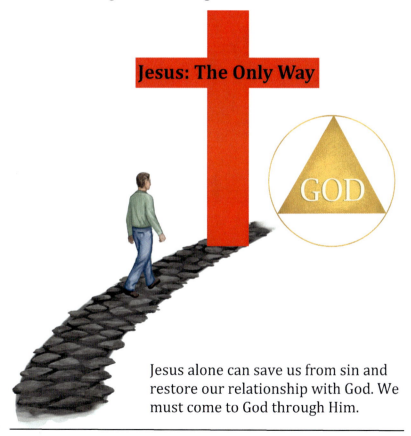

Jesus alone can save us from sin and restore our relationship with God. We must come to God through Him.

Acts 4:12: Nor is there salvation in any other, for there is no other name under heaven given among men by which we must be saved.

The Best Gift Ever

We can stay in the line of Adam or be **transferred** into the line of Christ, the Last Adam.

- Under God's dominion
- Receiving His forgiveness and righteousness
- Heading to eternal life

- Under Satan's dominion
- Holding onto our sin
- Heading to an eternal death

John 3:36: He who believes in the Son has everlasting life; and he who does not believe the Son shall not see life, but the wrath of God abides on him.

The Offer: The Great Exchange

We can choose Christ and all He offers.

Only a good God gives us choices, and they are always based on **Truth**.

This is the Truth:

- Jesus Christ died for our sins to give us forgiveness.

- Jesus Christ rose from the dead to give us His perfect righteousness.

- Jesus Christ ascended to heaven to give us His Holy Spirit.

Acts 5:30-32: The God of our fathers raised up Jesus whom you murdered by hanging on a tree. Him God has exalted to His right hand to be Prince and Savior, to give repentance to Israel and forgiveness of sins. And we are His witnesses to these things, and so also is the Holy Spirit whom God has given to those who obey Him.

The Best Gift Ever

In His mercy, God provided a remedy to rescue us from sin, death, and hell.

MERCY

Mercy is *not giving* us what we *do* deserve.

The Bible tells us that God has prepared a place called hell for the devil and his angels. It is described as a lake of fire. Those who choose to stay in the line of Adam and refuse God's gift are choosing to receive the same fate as Satan.

As with God's warning in the garden of Eden, this is not a threat! God is not hanging this lake of fire over our heads in condemnation. NO! Out of His great love, He is **warning** us. The Good News is that we don't have to go there! We don't have to stay in Adam's line.

God sent His Son Jesus Christ to take upon Himself all the pain, suffering, and punishment we deserve. God has done everything necessary to rescue us from sin, death, and hell. Because of His mercy, God has done everything necessary to provide a way back to Himself.

Ephesians 2:4-5: But God, who is rich in mercy, because of His great love with which He loved us, even when we were dead in trespasses, made us alive together with Christ...

The Offer: The Great Exchange

The cross, the resurrection, and the promise of His Spirit display both the mercy and the grace of God.

GRACE

Grace is *giving* us what we *don't* deserve.

In His grace, He offers us the best gift ever: The gift of new life within and all that goes with it. All we have to do is **accept** His free gift.

Mercy and grace are the climax of God's love. They are the highest and best demonstrations of His great love that looks beyond our sin-stained hearts, not only seeing our deep need, but also stooping down to meet that need.

Ephesians 2:6-9: ...(by grace you have been saved), and raised us up together, and made us sit together in the heavenly places in Christ Jesus, that in the ages to come He might show the exceeding riches of His grace in His kindness toward us in Christ Jesus. For by grace you have been saved through faith, and that not of yourselves; it is the gift of God, not of works, lest anyone should boast.

The Best Gift Ever

As God came to the first man and woman in the garden, so God seeks us out, calling us to return to Him.

RETURN

Restoring fellowship with God requires returning to Him in confession. Through confession, we are acknowledging that we need His forgiveness. As He did with Adam and Eve, God asks us the question, "What have you done?" He seeks to draw out into the open our personal sins. As specific sins come to mind, confess them to God. He knows all about them already, so nothing will shock Him. He has already died for them, so He won't reject us for them. **Admit** to God what you've done in disobedience against Him.

I John 1:9: If we confess our sins, He is faithful and just to forgive us our sins, and to cleanse us from all unrighteousness.

The Offer: The Great Exchange

A restored relationship also requires responding to God in faith.

RESPOND

When we **believe** in Jesus as our Savior from sin, we are making a trade. It is the bargain of the ages, a gift of grace. We give our sins to Jesus, acknowledging that He already bore the punishment for them on the cross. By accepting His forgiveness and receiving His perfect righteousness, we are made as right with God as Jesus is. When we make this exchange, no one can point an accusing finger at us before God for any of the sins we've done. Like someone putting money in our bank account that we didn't earn, God is counting Jesus' perfect obedience as if we had perfectly obeyed!

II Corinthians 5:21: For He [God the Father] made Him [Jesus the Son] who knew no sin to be sin for us, that we might become the righteousness of God in Him.

The Best Gift Ever

When we respond to Christ in faith, the same Spirit who enabled Jesus to fully obey God while here on earth, comes to dwell in our hearts. **Claim** Christ's promise to fill you with His Holy Spirit.

RECEIVE

His Holy Spirit

- gives life to our dead spirit,
- creates a new heart within us that wants to obey God,
- assures us from the inside that we are children of God,
- makes His salvation real to us day after day,
- gives us victory over sin, empowering us with the spiritual strength to say no to temptations,
- enables us to grow in our knowledge and understanding of God, of Jesus Christ, and of the salvation He has won for us.

Ezekiel 36:26-27: I will give you a new heart and put a new spirit within you; I will take the heart of stone out of your flesh and give you a heart of flesh. I will put My Spirit within you and cause you to walk in My statutes, and you will keep My judgments and do them.

The Offer: The Great Exchange

God helps us to **delight** in Him more and more each day by giving us specific ways to reinforce our decision to follow Christ.

- Read the Bible every day.

- Pray each day, worshipping God and giving your needs and cares to Him.

REINFORCE

- Surround yourself with godly people who will help you grow spiritually.
- Find a good Bible-teaching church.
- Share your new faith with others.

- Ask to be baptized as a public demonstration of the exchange you have made.

Matthew 28:19-20: Go therefore and make disciples of all the nations, baptizing them in the name of the Father and of the Son and of the Holy Spirit, teaching them to observe all things that I have commanded you…

The Best Gift Ever

When we receive the gift of salvation, our once-dead spirit is resurrected and comes alive again. We are **born anew**, or born of the Spirit. God calls light to shine out of the darkness within.

Then His Spirit begins a work within our spirit, training us how to live right-side-up again. Through our spirit connection with God, we learn to trust God's love for us and to believe that His commands are always good. Our growing faith in Him and His Word leads us to obedience. This ongoing work of God's Spirit in our hearts frees us from the dominating power of sin on a day-by-day basis. He trains us to base our thoughts, emotions, decisions, and actions on truth, empowering us to live according to what is pure and right.

The transformation of our whole spirit, soul, and body is a lifelong process.

I Thessalonians 5:23: Now may the God of peace Himself sanctify you completely; and may your whole spirit, soul, and body be preserved blameless at the coming of our Lord Jesus Christ. He who calls you is faithful, who also will do it.

The Offer: The Great Exchange

By thinking deeply and carefully about God's Word,

and by listening to His Spirit, which Christ places within our spirit,

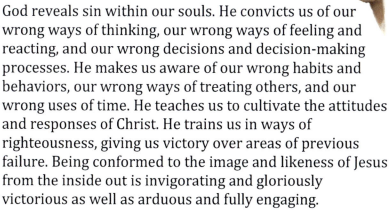

God reveals sin within our souls. He convicts us of our wrong ways of thinking, our wrong ways of feeling and reacting, and our wrong decisions and decision-making processes. He makes us aware of our wrong habits and behaviors, our wrong ways of treating others, and our wrong uses of time. He teaches us to cultivate the attitudes and responses of Christ. He trains us in ways of righteousness, giving us victory over areas of previous failure. Being conformed to the image and likeness of Jesus from the inside out is invigorating and gloriously victorious as well as arduous and fully engaging.

This is the journey of **sanctification**. As we become more and more like Christ, our whole being is set free from sin and becomes flooded with light as God originally designed.

II Corinthians 3:18: But we all, with unveiled face, beholding as in a mirror the glory of the Lord, are being transformed into the same image from glory to glory, just as by the Spirit of the Lord.

The Best Gift Ever

The Gospel, God's Good News, is a total **transformation** of

- Identity
- Focus
- Loyalty
- Commitment

It changes all of life.

The Gospel is not a one-time event that we can check off our list as done and move on.

The Gospel is not a ticket to heaven in our back pocket.

The Gospel is the power of God for complete, continual, and abundant salvation from sin to righteousness.

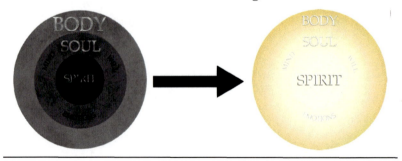

II Corinthians 5:17: Therefore, if anyone is in Christ, he is a new creation; old things have passed away; behold, all things have become new.

The Offer: The Great Exchange

Like a constantly flowing river of water, God pours His life into our lives, continually cleansing, renewing, and empowering us.

Live in the Truth of the **Gospel**. Draw from the wells of Gospel salvation that will never run dry.

Isaiah 12:3: Therefore with joy you will draw water from the wells of salvation.

John 7:37-38: On the last day, that great day of the feast, Jesus stood and cried out, saying, "If anyone thirsts, let him come to Me and drink. He who believes in Me, as the Scripture has said, out of his heart will flow rivers of living water."

An Invitation

If you have read through this book, you know there's a choice to be made. It's a choice of faith: to believe what's written in the Bible and to accept what God has offered, or to refuse to believe God's Word and turn away from the offer.

Perhaps you just don't want to bother with making a choice right now. But delay is also a choice of unbelief. None of us knows how long we have on this earth before death claims us. So I urge you not to fool yourself into thinking you can make this decision another time. That time may not come. As people often say, "Tomorrow never comes." We only have today. Putting off a decision as monumental as this until "a more convenient time" is one of Satan's favorite lures and biggest lies. And we know what he's after—the dominion of our souls. We also know how he hates God and us, and we know where following him leads us.

Or perhaps you don't know whether to believe it or not. That's certainly valid. If that's the case, don't simply set aside your questions to explore "someday." There's too much at stake, both for the present life here on earth and for eternity. (And that's a very long time!) "Someday" generally doesn't come. Other concerns and activities will

The Best Gift Ever

crowd out your search for God, and we too often postpone and neglect the things that are most important. That, too, is one of Satan's favorite tricks.

There are many good resources where you can find answers to your questions. Start with reading the Bible, and ask the God who made you and loved you enough to die for you to reveal Himself and make His truth known to you. He will do that if you ask. He wants to be known, and He longs to open the greatness of His loving heart to you. He also wants you to freely open your heart and life to Him.

Receiving God's free gift of righteousness is not difficult. It's as simple as receiving a gift.

- First of all, RETURN: by **A**dmitting to Him that you have a sin problem, that you can't cleanse yourself from sin, and that you need a Savior. Humbly confess your sins to God and receive His promised forgiveness.
- Second, RESPOND: by **B**elieving what Jesus Christ has done for you. Thank God for providing the *gift* of His very own righteousness. When you believe in Jesus as your Savior from sin, you are accepting the gift of His perfection.
- Third, RECEIVE: by **C**laiming the promise of His Holy Spirit. Commit your life to the Lord Jesus Christ and ask Him to fill you with His Holy Spirit who comes to live inside you when you make that exchange with God.

The Invitation

- Finally, after receiving the gift God offers you, REINFORCE: by **D**elighting in God in demonstrable ways:
  - Surround yourself with godly friends who will encourage you spiritually.
  - Find a good church that teaches the Bible and worships God.
  - Share the good news of what God has done for you with others.
  - Get baptized as a public testimony of your new life in Christ.
  - Read your Bible and pray everyday.

I pray you will make the decision to believe in Jesus. When you do, a whole new dimension will be added to your life. The course of your life will change direction. Everything may look the same on the outside, but you will be different on the inside. Your soul makes a shift from sin to righteousness. How you think, how you feel, how you make decisions, how you determine priorities, and how you relate to others begins to become God-centered rather than self-centered. The very Spirit of the living God comes to live inside of you. Like an internal personal Coach, He instructs, trains, encourages, and guides you each step of the way. He promises never to leave you or forsake you. The Word of God is your guide book for your new life. In relevant and practical ways, the Spirit will help you apply the truth of God's Word to situations in your daily life. He will give you the power to do all the things God calls you to do. He affirms all the promises of God, and He teaches you to trust His goodness, to rely on His strength, and to rest in His faithfulness and mercy.

Life will sometimes be difficult and painful. God never promised us an existence of ease and pleasure. But the lifelong process of learning to live our lives right-side up is a journey like no other. The best part of the journey is knowing and serving the God of the universe. He has promised to walk with us all the way. He is our constant Companion and Friend who will never leave us or forsake us. He is the One we can talk to about anything at any time. All of this is because of Jesus.

If you make a decision to receive God's gift of righteousness and all that comes with it, or if you have questions, please feel free to reach out to us via the addresses below. We'd love to hear from you.

Email: reservoirofgracefrp@gmail.com
Website: www.reservoirofgrace.com

Scripture References

Each page contains a primary Scripture reference. This index gives a few more Bible verses that pertain to each page. The references in bold type are the ones printed on the pages.

p. 3
John 17:17
Isaiah 33:5-6
Psalm 119:89, 130, 140, 151-152, 160
Psalm 18:30
Psalm 12:6-7
Proverbs 30:5-6

p. 4
II Peter 1:21
II Timothy 3:16

p. 5
Jeremiah 9:24
Numbers 23:19
Deuteronomy 32:3-4
Malachi 3:6
I John 4:8

The Best Gift Ever

John 5:39 (There are many verses throughout the Bible that tell us who God is and what His character is like. The verses revealing the character of God are so numerous that you should just read through the whole Bible!)

p. 6

Isaiah 46:9-10
Isaiah 40:12-14, 21-23, 25-26, 28
Genesis 2:4
Psalm 14:1

p. 8

Genesis 1:14-16
Genesis 1:26-27
Genesis 2:2-3
Genesis 2:18, 24
Genesis 2:16-17
Genesis 3

p. 9

Genesis 3:21
Genesis chapters 6-9
Genesis 7:12, 20, 24
Genesis 11:9

p. 10

Jeremiah 17:9
Romans 3:10, 19, 23
Romans 5:12

Scripture References

p. 11
Romans 11:36
Psalm 45:1-7, 10-12
Psalm 139:13-16
Isaiah 43:7
Isaiah 44:2
I Peter 2:9
Psalm 29:2

p. 12
Colossians 1:19-20
Ephesians 1:9-10
Mark 16:15

p. 15
Genesis 1:1
II Corinthians 13:14
Matthew 3:16-17; Luke 3:22
Genesis 1:26-27
Matthew 28:19
I Peter 1:2
I Corinthians 12:4-6

p. 16
Colossians 1:16
John 1:1-5
Hebrews 1:2
Psalm 148:1-6

p. 17
Genesis 1
Genesis 2:4

The Best Gift Ever

Psalm 33:6-9
Psalm 104
Isaiah 42:5
Isaiah 44:24
Isaiah 45:18
Isaiah 48:13
Isaiah 66:1-2
Jeremiah 10:12
Revelation 4:11

p. 18

Psalm 104:24
Psalm 97:6
Psalm 75:1
Psalm 95:6
Psalm 89:11
I Corinthians 8:6
Ephesians 4:4-6

p. 19

Psalm 111:2
Psalm 92:5
Revelation 4:11

p. 20

Psalm 45:6
Psalm 103:19
Psalm 95:1-5
Psalm 98:4
Psalm 99:1-3
Matthew 6:10

Scripture References

John 18:36
Acts 28:31
Romans 14:17
I Corinthians 6:9-10
Revelation 11:15

p. 21

I John 4:7-8
John 3:16
Psalm 117:2
Ephesians 3:17-19

p. 22

Genesis 2:7
Genesis 5:1-2
I Corinthians 15:21-22, 45-49

p. 23

Genesis 5:1-2
Genesis 1:26-27
Genesis 2:18-23
Luke 3:38

p. 24

I Thessalonians 5:23
Proverbs 20:27
Romans 8:1-16

p. 25

Genesis 1:28
Psalm 8:4-8 (Hebrews 2:6-8)

The Best Gift Ever

p. 29
Psalm 148:2, 5
Hebrews 1:13-14
Psalm 103:20
Daniel 6:22
Matthew 16:27
Matthew 18:10
Matthew 25:31
Luke 2:13-14
Luke 15:10
Revelation 5:11-12

p. 30
Isaiah 14:13-14
Luke 10:18
Ezekiel 28:12-19

p. 31
Revelation 12:3-4, 9
Luke 10:18

p. 32:
John 8:44
II Corinthians 11:14
John 10:10
I Peter 5:8

p. 35
Genesis 1:31
Genesis 2:9
I Chronicles 29:12
Psalm 16:11

Scripture References

Psalm 24:1
Psalm 103:19

pp. 36-37
Genesis 2:8-9, 15-17

p. 38
Deuteronomy 30:15-18
Romans 6:23
I John 3:4
I Corinthians 6:9-10
Galatians 5:19-21

p. 39
Genesis 2:9
Proverbs 3:5-6
Joshua 21:45
II Samuel 7:28
Psalm 119:151, 160
Psalm 19:8-9
John 18:37

pp. 40-41
Genesis 3:1, 14
I John 5:19
Ephesians 6:12
Revelation 12:9
Revelation 20:2

p. 42
Genesis 3:1
Genesis 2:9, 16

The Best Gift Ever

Psalm 31:19
Psalm 34:8
Psalm 107:8-9
Psalm 145:9

p. 43

Genesis 3:4-5
Genesis 1:26-27
Genesis 3:22

p. 44

Genesis 3:6
I Timothy 2:13-14

p. 45

Ephesians 2:1-3
James 1:13-15

p. 46

Genesis 3:7-8
Ezra 9:6
Jeremiah 17:13
I Peter 4:3
I John 2:16

p. 47

Genesis 3:9-10
Ephesians 4:17-19 (particularly verse 18)
Isaiah 59:2

p. 48

I John 1:9
Genesis 3:11-13

Proverbs 28:13
Acts 3:19
James 5:16

p. 51

Genesis 3:15
Revelation 21:4-6
Revelation 22:1-5

p. 52

Genesis 3:20
Isaiah 7:14
Isaiah 9:6-7
Galatians 4:4-5

p. 53

Genesis 3:21
Ezekiel 18:20b
Ezekiel 18:4

p. 54

Leviticus 17:11
Hebrews 9:22
Leviticus 4:27-30
Leviticus 5:5-6, 17-19

p. 55

Exodus 12:3, 5-7, 13
John 1:29
Exodus 12 (particularly verses 13-14)
Numbers 28:3-4
I Peter 1:18-20

The Best Gift Ever

p. 56
Romans 5:12
Genesis 3:16-19
Ezekiel 18:4
I Corinthians 15:21
Galatians 3:10
James 1:15
Revelation 21:4

p. 57
Genesis 3:24

p. 61
I John 5:19
John 14:30
Ephesians 2:2

p. 62
Romans 3:23
Romans 5:19
Isaiah 24:5-6
Romans 1:28-32
Romans 3:19
Romans 5:12, 14-21
Galatians 5:19-21
Ephesians 2:1-3
II Timothy 3:1-5
I Peter 4:3-4

Scripture References

p. 63

Isaiah 59:2
Genesis 5:5
Ephesians 2:3
Ephesians 4:17-19

p. 64

Romans 8:5-8, 13
Romans 7:7-24
Galatians 5:17-21

p. 65

I Corinthians 15:22
Psalm 51:5
Romans 5:12
Ephesians 2:1-3
James 1:14-15
I John 5:19

p. 66

Isaiah 53:6
Nehemiah 1:7
Romans 3:10-11, 19-23, 29
James 2:10-11

p. 69

I Peter 1:18-20
Romans 5:8
Isaiah 53:5, 8, 11-12

The Best Gift Ever

p. 70
Galatians 4:4
Luke 1:35
John 1:14, 18
John 3:16
I John 4:9

p. 71
Luke 1:31-32, 35
John 1:14, 18
John 3:16
Isaiah 7:14
Matthew 1:23
I Corinthians 15:45
Hebrews 1:2-3
Hebrews 2:17-18
Hebrews 4:15

p. 72
Matthew 1:21
John 1:1
Isaiah 7:14
Matthew 1:19-25
Colossians 2:9
John 10:30
John 14:9-11

p. 73
I Corinthians 15:45, 47
II Corinthians 5:21
Hebrews 4:15

Scripture References

Hebrews 7:26
I Peter 1:18-19

p. 74

John 4:25-26
Matthew 26:63-65
Mark 8:27-30
Luke 2:11
Acts 2:36

p. 75

John 4:42
Titus 2:13
I John 4:14

p. 76

Matthew 3:16
Mark 1:9-11
Luke 3:21-22

p. 77

Matthew 3:17
Mark 1:9-11
Luke 3:21-22

p. 78

I John 3:5
Hebrews 4:15
Matthew 26:64
Mark 10:45
John 12:23, 34-36
John 13:31

The Best Gift Ever

p. 79
John 8:29
John 5:19-30, 36, 43
John 6:38
John 7:16
John 8:26, 28-29, 38, 42, 50
John 10:25, 37-38
John 12:49

p. 80
John 10:11, 17-18
I Peter 1:18-19
Isaiah 53:5-6
Matthew 26:39, 42
John 1:29
Philippians 2:8
Revelation 5:6-13

p. 81
Acts 2:23-24
John 5:28-29
Romans 6:9
Romans 6:23
II Timothy 1:10
Revelation 22:14-15

p. 82
Matthew 28:18
John 12:31
Colossians 2:15
Hebrews 2:14-15

Scripture References

I Peter 2:24
Revelation 20:10

p. 83
Daniel 7:13-14
Daniel 2:44
Daniel 4:34
Daniel 6:26
Daniel 7:27
I Corinthians 15:25-26
Revelation 11:15
Revelation 19:6
Revelation 21:3-5, 22-27

p. 84
Luke 24:51
John 16:7
John 14:16-18
Acts 1:4-11

p. 87
II Corinthians 5:19
Romans 5:1-2, 11
II Corinthians 5:18, 20
Galatians 6:14
Ephesians 2:16
Colossians 1:19-20

p. 88
Romans 5:10
Matthew 27:46, Mark 15:34

The Best Gift Ever

II Corinthians 5:18, 20
Galatians 3:13
Ephesians 1:7
Ephesians 2:13
Colossians 1:19-20
I Timothy 2:5
Hebrews 2:17 (propitiation is the sacrificial act of a mediator that brings reconciliation between the one who is offended and the offender)
I Peter 1:18-19
I John 2:1-2
I John 4:10

p. 89

Romans 5:17
Acts 16:30-31
John 6:28-29
Romans 4:5
Romans 5:1
Romans 10:9-10
Ephesians 1:3-6
Ephesians 4:24

p. 90

Colossians 1:13
Acts 26:18
Romans 6:14
Hebrews 2:14-15
I Peter 2:9-10

Scripture References

p. 91

John 1:12-13
Romans 8:14-17
Galatians 4:4-7
Ephesians 1:3-5
Colossians 2:13
I John 3:1-2

p. 92

Ephesians 1:7
Exodus 34:6-7
Psalm 103:8-12
Micah 7:18-19
Romans 4:7-8
Colossians 1:14
I Peter 2:24

p. 93

Romans 4:25-5:1
Isaiah 53:11
Romans 3:21-26
Romans 4:5
Romans 5:16-21
Romans 8:1

p. 94

John 14:16-17
Philippians 2:13
Luke 24:49
John 16:7, 13
Romans 5:5

The Best Gift Ever

Romans 8:3-6, 11, 13-16, 26
Galatians 3:3
Galatians 5:22-23
Ephesians 1:13-14

p. 97
Deuteronomy 30:19-20
John 3:36
Romans 10:11-13

p. 98
Joshua 24:15
John 8:44
Revelation 12:9
Revelation 20:7-8, 10

p. 99
Acts 4:12
John 14:6
Acts 4:10
Acts 16:31
Colossians 1:19-20
I Timothy 2:5

p. 100
John 3:36
John 3:18
I John 3:8, 10, 14-15

p. 101
Acts 5:30-32
Acts 2:36, 38

Scripture References

I Corinthians 15:3-4
Acts 1:4-11

p. 102

Ephesians 2:4-5
Psalm 103:11
Psalm 36:5
Matthew 13:41-42
Matthew 25:41, 46
John 5:29
John 8:24
Revelation 20:14-15
Revelation 21:6-8
Revelation 22:14-15

p. 103

Ephesians 2:6-9
John 1:16-17
Romans 5:20-21
Titus 2:11-14
Hebrews 4:15-16

p. 104

I John 1:9
Psalm 32:1-5
Proverbs 28:13
Isaiah 55:7
Hosea 14:1-2
Acts 2:38-39

The Best Gift Ever

Acts 3:19-20
II Corinthians 7:10

p. 105

II Corinthians 5:21
I Corinthians 6:9-11
Ephesians 1:3-8
Hebrews 10:22
I Peter 2:24

p. 106

Ezekiel 36:26-27
Acts 2:38
Romans 6:11-13
Titus 2:11-14

p. 107

Matthew 28:19-20
Psalm 119:9, 11, 105
Acts 2:38
Hebrews 4:12
Ephesians 6:18
Colossians 4:2
I Thessalonians 5:17
I Timothy 2:1
II Timothy 3:14-17
Hebrews 10:23-25

p. 108

I Thessalonians 5:23
John 17:15-19

Scripture References

Romans 6:11-13, 19
I Corinthians 15:49
II Corinthians 4:6
Philippians 2:12-13
I Thessalonians 4:3-5
Titus 2:11-14
I Peter 1:14-16
I John 3:1-3

p. 109

II Corinthians 3:18
II Timothy 2:15
John 10:27
Romans 8:13-14
John 16:7-11
Romans 8:29
Romans 12:2
II Timothy 3:16-17

p. 110

II Corinthians 5:17
Romans 1:16-17
Romans 12:1-2
I Peter 1:3-9

p. 111

Isaiah 12:3
John 7:37-38
Psalm 36:8-9
John 4:14

Acknowledgements

I am very grateful to all who made this book better with your many helpful suggestions and corrections: Jan Lehmann, Tina Burt, Donna Steinbrugge, David and Marianne Boone, Kea Hufford, Jenny Crichton, Richard Cole, Evan Humphreys, Sheryl Endicott. If I have forgotten anyone, please forgive me. Beyond the actual making of this book, God knows there are many over the years who have shaped this message in my soul.

A special thanks to Ruth Posthuma for your line-by-line editing skills and for taking so much time to go over it with me; to Sally Carpenter for checking all the Scripture references, a long and tedious job; and to my daughter, Tirzah, for your patience and skill in formatting and reformatting through multiple revisions. I cannot thank you all enough!

Made in the USA
Middletown, DE
19 December 2023